A Beginne
Mountaii

Gieven in Memory

of

Nancy Keenen O'Neil

Achim Schmidt

A Beginner's Guide
Mountain
Biking

Meyer & Meyer Sport

Original title: Tipps für Mountainbiking
© Meyer & Meyer Verlag, Aachen 2003
Translated by Anne Lammert

British Library Cataloguing in Publication Data
A catalogue record for this book is available from the British Library

Schmidt, Achim:
A Beginner's Guide
Mountain Biking
Oxford: Meyer & Meyer Sport (UK) Ltd., 2004
ISBN 1-84126-146-7

© 2004 by Meyer & Meyer Sport (UK) Ltd.
Aachen, Adelaide, Auckland, Budapest, Graz, Johannesburg, .
Miami, Olten (CH), Oxford, Singapore, Toronto
Member of the World
Sports Publishers' Association (WSPA)
www.w-s-p-a.org
Printed and bound by: FINIDR, s. r. o., Český Těšín
ISBN 1-84126-146-7
E-Mail: verlag@m-m-sports.com
www.m-m-sports.com

CONTENTS

1 BUYING A BIKE

1,000 $ for a mountain bike? Well if it has to cost so much it should at least be worth the investment!

Buying the first mountain bike can pose quite a problem for any newcomer, due to the large range on offer and the lack of necessary specialist knowledge. In order to be able to follow a sales assistant's explanations it is generally wise to have had a good look through all the latest specialist magazines in the weeks beforehand. Basic terms and all the technicalities will be explained and clarified in these publications. With this basic knowledge of *technical cycling* you can then get down to business with the salesman. Anyone requiring current test data on the latest brakes, gear systems and forks can find ample reading material in the MTB specialist journals. A word of warning however: do not attach too much importance to these results as they are not always completely objective.

1.1 Some Advice on Buying

The price of the bike of your dreams may appear to be high, but in general this price illustrates the bike's high quality. It is possible to buy a new, functionable bike at a discount store or in a DIY store. However, you're not going to have more than one summer of cross-country fun with it. Anyone who thinks he's made a great bargain with a bike providing full suspension and disc braking for 400 $ will soon notice that this was an illusion. In short: anyone who does a lot of biking will have to spend that much more in order to attain long-term enjoyment out of it.

Important: Each high-quality 'special extra' (suspension etc) will send this price upward. A bike with all the features, described above, is only available at a reasonable price because the quality of its components is well under average standard. It is possible to buy a bike of acceptable quality for 600 $, however, it lacks in technical finesse and weighs a bit more as well. "No problem", you may think, "It's exactly the right thing for my purpose!". You're right, but have a closer look at what your purpose is. If you'd like to have the odd extra, the price quickly reaches 1,000 $. Bikes which are high in quality cost at least 1,500 $ and there is hardly an upper limit here. A higher price does not imply that the level of quality increases in the same proportion. When it comes down to it, from a price range of 2,000 $ upward, one must pay an excessively high price for each gram of weight saved.

Watch out for Certain Details!

With some background information and the right tips and advice it is very easy to test a bike's quality yourself. Even if you don't end up being an absolute expert on all matters it will, however, enable you to separate the wheat from the chaff. It is not easy to differentiate between high-quality parts and cheap ones. Several manufacturers copy the appearance of high-quality components and it is often the case that hidden details such as pedal bearings, hubs or the A-Head are anything but high in quality.

The Right Place to Buy

From the list of manufacturers in the Internet it is usually possible to pick out a nearby store. Needless to say, this is equally possible using the classical telephone method. Discount stores and department stores seldom provide good service, as their sales assistants only occasionally possess the necessary specialist knowledge.

How can I tell if a bike dealer is good or not? First of all by his competence in being able to clearly explain the advantages and particularly the disadvantages of certain components and innovations. His arguments should be plausible, i.e understandable and convincing, without being too persuasive. Not everything that is new and espensive suits your requirements.

A good specialist store distinguishes itself by the possibility of having a test ride, individual adjustments and the replacement of certain parts when necessary, and not by 'freebies'. A free of charge initial inspection is something not to be underestimated. High quality bikes are largely developed from a technical point of view and require specialized maintenance at regular intervals. Needless to say, this service does not come free of charge, but the product's durability is your profit.

Be Careful in DIY Stores!

Yet another few words on DIY stores etc: the bikes look good and the technical features appear acceptable for such an attractive price. However, the low price implies a certain risk. Several components may look good, but will only hold out a few kilometers. In many cases it is impossible to get spare parts and there is no real service in the first place.

1.2   Frame and Fork

The frame, as the 'heart' of the bike, is of special significance. On the one hand it distributes the cyclist's weight on both wheels and on the other hand it is the point of assembly for all of the additional parts. Therefore, it has to be robust and stable but at the same time should not be too hard so that it offers a certain level of comfort when cycling.

Hardtail or Fully

When a couple of freaks brought the mountain bike to life in the mountains of San Francisco in the 1970s, nobody was thinking about the possibility of suspension. The so-called **Rigid Bikes,** with their stiff, rigid forks and no suspension, were the bikes that were used then.

Illustration 1.1: Hardtails are light and 'stiff' (here the 'Team Issue', 9.5 kg)

Nowadays, nearly all bikes have a fork with suspension. A bike with suspension fork is referred to as a **Hardtail** due to the rear of the bike having no suspension. A bike with both suspension fork and springs at the rear is a **full suspension bike**, for short **'Fully'**. The **Hardtail** is an all-round bike and can be put to use almost everywhere. A **Fully** was originally developed for downhill use. The greater suspension enables much faster and safer downhill cycling than with a bike having no suspension.

Technical Progress Is Unstoppable

New and improved suspension systems for bikes have constantly been developed in the past few years. As a result the differences in purpose between the Hardtail and the Fully have become increasingly blurred. The so-called **Cross-country Fullies** are light, stable and are excellently suited for all those areas of use provided by the classic hardtail. A Fully of equal value, however, costs a good bit more, but then provides more cycling comfort and overall safety. If it is not possible to lock a Fully's rear suspension, uphill cycling can become a torture as the bike drifts away under the cyclist from one side to the other, particularly in the rocking position. Latest technology has proved to be on the right track here though. An absorbing element which 'thinks along' with the bike, remains completely hard on hard surfaces and offers suspension on rough surfaces.

Illustration 1.2: Modern Fullies are getting lighter and better all the time (11.0kg)

All for the Sake of Our Health

Suspension on a bike makes sense, particularly for frequent biking on poor surfaces or cross-country. For example, the strain to the spinal column on bad surfaces is reduced by about a third and our body has to carry out less holding and supporting work on bumpy roads. Anyone with back problems can only benefit from the bike's suspension when he combines this by adapting a suitable, erect sitting position at the same time.

The bikers themselves are meanwhile divided in opinion. On the one hand we have the Hardtail purists who don't reject the Fullies, but still prefer to feel the Hardtail's direct drive, and on the other hand the growing group of Fully fans, springing through the woods. The following table summarizes the advantages and disadvantages of both frame types so that each biker can decide for himself what bike is ideal for him.

	Hardtail	Fully
Cost	+	–
Weight	+	–
Comfort	–	+
Maintenance Requirements	0	+
Rear	0	–
Construction Wear & Tear	+	–
Uphill	+	–
		With lockout 0
Downhill	0	+

Illustration 1.3: Hardtail vs Fully (+ advantage, – disadvantage)

Geometry

Bar angle and bar length determine a frame's geometry. As opposed to racing bikes, there are many different frame constructions for mountain bikes. Apart from those genuine improvements on detail, there is also an entire series of marketing-based constructions, the advantages of which are not always related to good cycling techniques.

11

Long Live the Diamond Frame!

The Diamond frame is the oldest but certainly the most tried and tested geometrical form of frame construction around. Despite numerous attempts with other geometrical forms and various different materials, the Diamond frame remains the bike frame of the future. Made up of 11 bars, assembled into a triangle (rear construction) and a square (front construction), the Diamond frame is known for its very high vertical stiffness and a significantly lower sideward stiffness. The latter is a problem, which engineers have been working on for years with only moderate success. The sideward stiffness provided by the leading bike manufacturers is sufficient in most cases.

Most bike frames make use of the so-called **sloping geometry**, whereby the top bar slopes downward toward the saddle. In this way it is possible to build frames smaller and stiffer.

Illustration 1.4: The mountain bike and its components

Alu or...?

It is not really necessary to ask the question whether aluminum or another material, as apart from carbon there is no other material that is used to such a significant amount. Aluminum is used more than 99% of the time.

What distinguishes aluminum is its low weight. However, as it is not as firm as steel for example, the tube walls must be thicker and the tube diameter larger, and still the frame ends up being lighter than a normal steel frame. Aluminum frames are welded and are available in several different geometrical styles.

Illustration 1.5: Alu-frames are light, sturdy and reasonably priced

The raw material carbon has an extremely high elasticity and a very low specific weight. The individual carbon fibers, however, have to be connected with a resin, which reduces the elasticity and raises the weight. An improvement in glueing techniques (glued frames) and the lining up of the weaves according to the lines of force (Monocoque) has enabled the construction of very good frames, which, however, are also more expensive. As opposed to alu-frames, carbon frames are significantly more prone to scratches and dents on cross-country rides. Carbon frames do have one significant advantage, however: they dampen vibrations and bumpiness better than other frames – they provide more comfort.

Frame Size

The frame size determines your choice of frame and it is important that this fits the body size. The frame height is measured from the middle of the pedal bearing housing up to the top of the saddle tube and is given in inches or centimeters. Some manufacturers have their frames labelled with XS-XXL sizes, which corresponds to normal clothing sizes incredibly well. There are far fewer frame sizes for mountain bikes available than for racing bikes, but this can be compensated for by using saddle tubes and stems available in several lengths.

The following table shows the frame height according to body height, and should serve as a rough guide only. Smaller frames are the trend today, which means one goes for a frame suitable for a shorter person. Frame height is determined by the length of your leg in particular. A person with short legs should thus go for a frame which is actually slightly too short for him.

Body Height	Size	ins	cm
< 165 cm	XS	14,5	36
163-170 cm	S	16	40
169-178 cm	M	17,5	44
176-185 cm	L	19	48
183-194 cm	XL	20,5	52
> 195 cm	XXL	22	56

Illustration 1.6: Frame sizes

Women normally choose a frame 1–2cm smaller than a man of the same size, as their upper body is often shorter in relation to their legs. A shorter frame gives a significantly more comfortable position. For example *Scott USA* has the so-called **Solution Geometry** for women based on the criteria above. Bikes intended for racing have longer frames, which permit a more stretched position.

For youths and teenagers it is recommended to buy a frame that is slightly too big to allow for growth. Large and heavy bikers are better cycling with a sturdier and thus heavier frame. They should stay away from constructions using thinly made tubing to ensure sufficient sideward stiffness and good durability even with a big frame.

Another significant criterion for the correct frame size is, as already mentioned, the frame length. Buying a frame off the peg however, allows hardly any scope for differences in lengths; one merely has the possibility of choosing between different brand names, which may offer various lengths.

Suspension

Many cheap suspension systems hardly dampen at all and are soon worn out. The poor suspension is then gone completely and the biker ends up trailing this extra weight along with him.

For this reason one should pay attention to products of a reputable firm e.g., *Rock Shoxx*, *Marzocchi* or *Magura* when choosing fork suspension or rear suspension. The more reasonably priced, sprung saddle columns are an alternative to frame suspension (Fully).

Component Jargon

This brief advice on buying cannot help to clear the jungle of terms presented by all the components. However, a simple ranking among the manufacturers offers some light on the subject. *Shimano* provides mountain bike sets which are often assembled onto trekking bikes.

The set here refers to the gear changes and braking components. The second largest component manufacturer SRAM produces mainly MTB gear-changing sets, which can also be assembled onto trekking bikes.

By categorizing them according to classes, it is easy to allocate a value to each group. However, you can seldom buy a complete set, component *'mixes'* are more commonly available. This hinders a clear view of a bike's value enormously as the normal amateur can't keep up with all the different names anyway.

Categorization: 1 Newcomer, 2 Middle Class, 3 Upper Class, 4 Top Class									
Shimano	**1**	**2**	**3**	**4**	**SRAM**	**1**	**2**	**3**	**4**
XTR				x	9.0SL				x
Deore XT			x		9.0			x	
Deore LX			x		7.0		x		
Deore		x			5.0		x		
Alivio		x			4.0	x			
Acera	x				3.0	x			
Altus	x								
Tourney	x								

Illustration 1.7: Components (Shimano, SRAM)

1.3 Gear Changing Systems

The gear change adapts the gear ratio according to the different type of terrain and performance ability. Due to the many innovations in the past few years it is possible to comfortably change gears today working with 24-27 gears. Nine cogs are standard nowadays. A wide spectrum of possibilities is covered with such a great number of gears available. It is possible to ride both up and down extremely steep hills with the appropriate gear ratio. At the front there are three chain discs with mostly 42, 32 and 22 teeth and at the back nine cog wheels with 11-32 teeth. As opposed to racing bikes there is not much variation here as the gear ratio covers a wide span. With the *Shimano*, gears are changed using a total of four levers (Rapidfire) activated by press and pull movements. The SRAM has a trigger dial which is easy to operate.

The chain provides power transmission and together with the tires and brake pads is the most important wear-and-tear part on the bike; it is exposed to a good deal of pressure from the forces on it and dirt thus causing high wear. After about 2,000-6,000km the chain, depending on its quality and use, even when looked after well, will have done its duty. It should be replaced in order to avoid unnecessary wear with other moving parts.

1.4   Braking

An absolute essential requirement for safety when mountain biking is good brakes. The braking system consists of brake levers mounted on the handlebars, the brake cables, which activate the brakes, the brake cantilevers themelves and finally the wheel rim, on which the brake pads rub. The left braking lever activates the front wheel brake and this brake effect accounts for about two thirds of the total brake effect. The right brake lever is responsible for the rear wheel. A significant criterion of a brake's quality is its dosing measure; a strong pull of the brake should not cause an immediate blocking of the wheels. The force must be passed on to the brake rather in the right dosage in order to be able to carry out smooth and gentle braking.

Illustration 1.8: Disc brakes have a strong grip but are difficult to maintain

One differs between **mechanical** brakes, as mentioned above, and **hydraulic** brakes where the cable is 'replaced' by hydraulic oil. Discs and wheel rim brakes *(V brakes)* are available in both forms. The table offers information on the individual features.

Tip Even the reasonably priced brakes of the two major component manufacturers fulfill the above-mentioned demands and are by all means suitable for cross-country.

	Mechanical V-Brake	Mechanical Disc Brake	Hydraulic V-Brake	Hydraulic Disc Brake
Price	1	2	2	3
Weight	1	3	2	3
Dosage	Good	Good	Good	Good
Maintenance	Simple	Specialist	Specialist	Specialist
Max. Braking Performance	1	2	2	3

Illustration 1.9: Summary of Braking Systems (Ranking 1-3)

1.5   Wheels

Here we speak of the wheel of the mountain bike, which is made up of hub, spokes, wheel rim and tire. Wheels are a genuine technical wonder; while individually consisting of quite weak components, as a complex structure they form an extremely sturdy and nevertheless light wheel. A good wheel can take a weight of up to 500kg without losing its shape permanently.

The **hubs** form the centre of the wheel. They hold the tops of the spokes and form the connection to the frame. The ease of spinning is determined specifically by the free movement in the hub bearings: The most commonly used ball bearings are tapered ones where the balls turn within a layer of grease. For a good while now manufacturers have moved over to making the hubs from industrial bearings, which require no maintenance and prove to be very durable. Such hubs distinguish themselves by their silky soft running and which are extremely low in friction. They are well able to withstand muddy biking treatment.

The **spokes**, somewhat delicate on their own, are capable of standing an enormous amount of force under tension and they carry the weight of the cyclist. A normal wheel consists of 36 or 32 spokes; each of them crosses over three other ones. The 2mm double thick-ended spokes have proved to be successful, with a diameter of 1.6mm in the middle. Thanks to this tapering in the middle the spokes become more elastic and are less likely to snap. The critical point of a spoke is at the elbow end of the spoke, the position where the spoke is fitted into the hub flange. This is where most spokes snap.

A **rim** can be defined as a metal strip, which has been bent to form a circle – mostly made out of an aluminum alloy that is joined together at the so-called 'seam joint'. A well-finished seam is an absolute must for wheel rims of high quality. A rim's durability and sturdiness is closely connected to its weight and geometrical measurements (width, height, thickness of the sidewall). Thus an extremely light rim can never compete with a heavy rim as far as robustness and long life are concerned. On the other hand this does not mean that a rim should be as heavy as possible. Cyclists weighing 80kg and more are better cycling with heavier rims in the long term. The optimal rim for mixed purposes is a hard, anodized rim shaped in the form of a droplet. The high vertical stiffness prevents the rim from flattening when turning, the spokes are subjected to less strain and it is almost impossible for them to break.

> With V brakes, pay attention that the brake pads and the sides of the rim are clean in order to keep the rim's wear and tear down to a minimum. Rim sides do not wear out with disc brakes. **Tip**

A lot of importance is attached in selecting the right **tire** for mountain bike racing. The tire is selected following an inspection of the course; the trend in the cross-country these days is geared toward 'less tread' and a 'large cross-section'.

The tires make contact with the ground and determine the grip or possibility of sliding. An all-round biker is best off cycling with a thick tire with moderate tread.

Fast Fred   **Fat Albert**

Flat tread for high speed

Strong studs: grip and self-cleaning

Illustration 1.10: A modern MTB tire is significantly lighter than its predecessor of many years ago

As regards tire pressure, it is advisable to heed the manufacturer's instructions. The general basic rule is that one should only cycle with extremely high pressures when a low level of resistance is required (races) or when there is a high risk of puncturing (stones).

Otherwise, however, our back and joints are allowed a somewhat higher level of comfort and we can have our tires pumped up at a lower pressure. They are still able to roll well enough. The fact is though, that most bikers go training with far too little air pressure and thus end up with punctures, which could be avoided.

1.6   Saddle

The mountain bike saddle is one of three connection points between man and machine. It carries significantly more body weight than the handlebars. Just how important a good saddle is, is something you will mostly notice when it's too late.

Narrow saddles with particularly narrow noses are used in sports biking and prevent chafing of the thigh by the saddle. The saddle is stretched out over the saddle frame, which is made of steel, titanium or aluminum. As they don't need to be 'worn in', and because they are less sensitive to rain, plastic saddles are almost exclusively used nowadays with a leather or synthetic cover. Various layers of cushioning lie above the saddle's plastic shell – some manufacturers also use gel inlays. There are extremely light saddles (even of carbon) available, although the reduction in weight nearly always goes hand in hand with a diminshed level of comfort and less durability.

Illustration 1.11: The anatomically formed gel cushions distribute the pressure across a wider surface. In this way seating problems can be prevented ("Selle Royal")

A saddle should not be too soft as cycling is more comfortable on a harder saddle in the long term. Anatomically formed saddles have special cushioning for each side of the ishium and a special groove for the urethra. Shorter, slightly wider saddles are available for women, which accommodate the female anatomy.

Downhillers use very long saddles, which enable a change in sitting position depending on the type of ground.

In the end you can only find out the optimal saddle for you when you have already tried many beforehand, and from then on you will never change. A spring suspended saddle post can contribute a lot to overall comfort.

Tip

1.7 Pedalling Systems

Since the revolution in the pedal market, thanks to the company *Look* in 1985, a lot of progress has been made. At that time there was one sole supplier, today there are many firms extolling their various pedalling systems.

The safety pedal forms the basis of all pedalling systems on today's market: in the case of a fall the cyclist's feet must be automatically released from the pedal in order to avoid serious injuries. As well as this, it should be as easy as possible to get in and out of the pedals.

An adaptor under the shoe clicks into the built-in gap in the pedal by means of a locking mechanism. A twisting movement of the foot disengages this connection. The previous models, the totally stiff pedal-shoe connectors with a hook and straps, hinder the natural rotating movements of the lower leg when pedalling, which in turn can lead to difficulties with the knees and other joints.

The company *Time* developed a pedalling system, which gives your feet the necessary freedom of movement. Most of the professionals prefer this system. Only when a certain angle has been exceeded (5° in either direction) does the pedal unlock.

This anatomic and logical idea has gradually been copied by several other manufacturers. As well as this, it is perfectly easy to click in and out of this system, even in very muddy conditions.

Illustration 1.12: Shoes and pedals must fit each other. The "Time system" is considered to be particularly ergonomic (kind to joints and tendons)

Tip

> Athletes with orthopedic leg problems should use a pedalling system where the foot has sideward freedom of movement and with a sole-pedal difference that is as short as possible.

1.8   Accessories

The bike computer can be used not only for training documentation but also to a limited extent for training control. It shows the number of kilometers already covered, the speed, the duration of training and several other practical data for training or a race, all of which can be entered into a training diary at home.

You should best select an appliance where two or more items of information can be read simultaneously and which is easy to operate.

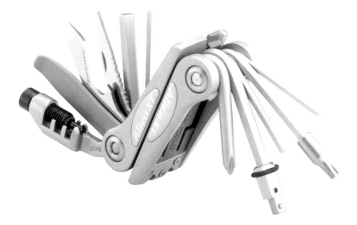

On a training ride a small bicycle pump is just as important a part of basic equipment as a reserve tube and a puncture repair kit .

Illustration 1.13: A minipump and "multifunctional tools" are indispensable when problems set in

Small repairs can be carried out on route with the so-called *multi-functional tool*.

Light mudguards can be mounted in seconds and dismounted again in good weather. These keep your clothes not only clean, but dry in particular.

Illustration 1.14: Tires can be pumped up easily at home with an upright pump

Illustration 1.15: Super-light mudguards

Anyone who needs to transport luggage should buy a special carrier for the saddle support bar and attach a travelling bag onto it.

Illustration 1.16: Transport luggage easily and steadily with the 'beam rack'

2   CYCLING CLOTHING

Sun, steep climbs, icy descents, wet lake crossings, thunder and storms are just a few of the weather conditions, which can set in on a single mountain bike tour. Only with special functional clothing will biking remain enjoyable, as our body is then protected from the weather in an appropriate way. Colds due to undercooling can be avoided so easily and effectively.

The following chapter deals with the most important features of optimally functioning MTB clothing.

Onion Skin Principle

Basically one should dress oneself for biking according to the onion skin principle. Several thin layers with various functions guarantee an optimal climate for the skin and the necessary protection from the weather. As well as this, the individual layers are very thin and light, thanks to modern materials. They are, therefore, comfortable to wear. If a layer is no longer required it can be taken off and stored in the tricot pockets (e.g. windproof top or detachable sleeves).

2.1   Underwear which Can 'Breathe'

There's nothing as uncomfortable as a sweaty cotton undershirt, which sticks to your skin and makes you freeze and shiver on a downhill ride. Regardless of the temperatures outside, racing cyclists always wear a special breathing undershirt next to their skin. This top is made of synthetic fibres and in contrast to cotton underwear, absorbs very little moisture. Thanks to its special structure, it transfers any sweat on the skin onto the next layer of clothing. Thus the skin stays much drier than with other shirts, which is something that is clearly noticeable through the higher skin temperature. Particularly in cooler weather this special undershirt always feels dry and warm.

When the temperatures go above 30°, some athletes go without functional underwear, but even then only when there aren't any long downhill stretches planned. Functional underwear does not feel uncomfortable in hot weather. Not only that, it's also much more pleasant on the skin than a tricot.

Polyamide or polyester are the materials that are suitable here. The basis of all models is a three-dimensional net structure, which increases the condensation surface. Unfortunately some manufacturer's materials tend to take on a musty smell. A good undershirt will cost you between 25 and 40 $, an amount that is definitely worth the investment and which rewards you with fewer colds throughout the year.

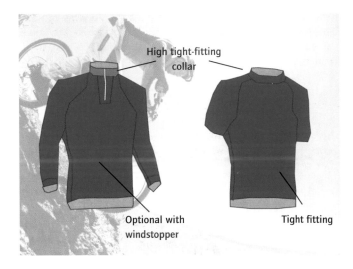

Illustration 2.1: A functional undershirt is just as important as a tricot, one should not make false economies here. Cotton absorbs more than 10 times as much moisture as special functional material

Undershirts come wihout sleeves, with short and long sleeves and with or without a high collar. It is also possible to buy them with a sewed-on wind-resistant protective layer, a so-called *"windbreaker"*. These undershirts can be recommended for in the mountains and during the winter.

2.2 Tricot

The next layer over the undershirt is the tricot. 20 years ago these tricots were made of cotton only, nowadays tricots are made of various different synthetic fibres. As a result the tricot, similar to the undershirt, absorbs only very little sweat and doesn't soak up all the moisture.

Thicker tricot materials, often with a napped inside, are intended for cold days, thin materials are suitable for hot weather. Tricots with a long zip from the top to the bottom enable the necessary cool breeze to get through on hot days, do bear the risk of trapping insects inside, however.

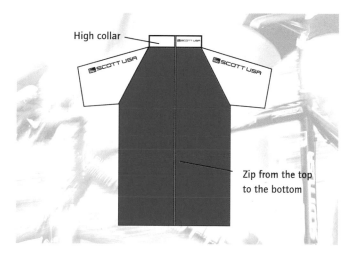

High collar

Zip from the top to the bottom

Illustration 2.2: The tricot should be tight-fitting and of 'breathing' material

A good fit is also important: particularly in the back it should not be too short so that the kidneys are well protected. A tricot should be tight-fitting and should not flutter in the wind. Casual tricots are also manufactured for the MTB area, however, they have a much wider fitting but are still made out of the same functional materials. If a tricot is too loosely, the airstream drifts in through the collar, causing cooling and especially undercooling of the upper body. Whichever shape of tricot you go for is all a matter of taste in the end.

Sewed on pockets at the back are handy for storing a rainproof, energy bars and keys. Long-sleeved tricots are available for cold weather as well as tricot jackets with a long zip.

Tip

On colder days one wears another tricot or fleece polo-neck under the tricot jacket or in very cold weather under the winter jacket.

2.3 Cycling Pants

Cycling pants are different to other sports pants due to a leather crotch lining, which is still referred to as *leather* but which is made of an easy-care textile fabric. This lining prevents sore chafing of the bottom, cushions it somewhat and protects it from the cold. This is thanks to the terry lining at the front. Racing pants should be close-fitting, shouldn't fall in folds and should not pinch anywhere.

Pants with braces are always more recommendable than those without as they also cover the kidney area, thus protecting them from the cold. Pants with braces do pose a problem, however, for women when a quick visit to the toilet is needed. Braces, which can be buttoned open or simply pants without braces can be of assistance here.

Mountain bikers also like cycling with very loose-fitting pants with pockets on the side, but these also have an inside tight pant with the above mentioned features fitted.

Braces guarantee a good fit

Sewed out of eight strips

Synthetic
leather for
sitting comfort

Few folds

SCOTT USA

Illustration 2.3: The pants are the most important piece of clothing for a cyclist

Pants with extra sewed-in cushioning and protectors are available for downhillers.

If possible, cycling pants should be washed after every training session in order to prevent any germs that stem from the leather being rubbed into the bottom; this can result in skin inflammation in this area.

For the winter months it is possible to buy three-quarter length pants and long pants both with braces. Thicker materials, which are napped on the inside are mostly used for long pants. Long pants with a built-in membrane at the front can be recommended for very cold weather. These are not as flexible as normal pants, but are very warm as well as windproof at the front.

A pair of pants sewed out of six or eight strips of material has a better shape and fit than one made up with only four strips. **Tip**

2.4   Shoes

Biking is much more enjoyable with MTB shoes, and the downforce when pedalling is more economical with them as well.

There is a choice between shoes with a heavily treaded sole and screw studs as well as shoes with ligher treading and a less stiffer sole. The more sporty the biking is, the stiffer the sole should be. High-quality MTB shoes have an extremely stiff sole, mostly synthetic (with carbon or metal inlays), and these help to optimize the downforce from the foot onto the pedal. Under the sole is a little plate for clicking into the pedal. This is an essential requirement for rounded pedalling. It is also no problem to cover long distances on foot with MTB shoes. They should be a little tighter than normal shoes so they have a good grip when pushing and pulling on the pedal. The upper material is made of synthetic leather (dries quickly) in combination with various synthetic sections for airing the shoe.

Illustration 2.4: A good shoe has an extremely stiff sole, which is still light in weight and has strong treading

Lately, velcro and rip fastenings have become more and more popular.

> Wet shoes dry best when you fill them with newspaper and **Tip**
> change this paper once a few hours later.

2.5   Helmet

It is absolutely important to wear a helmet to protect oneself from serious injuries. About 80% of all fractures of the base of the skull could be avoided if the athletes wore hard-top helmets. The risk of injury, particularly through mountain biking, is much higher than when cycling on a racing bike on the road. Numerous obstacles in the forest such as trees and rocks can lead to serious injuries in the case of a fall.

A hard top helmet must fit tightly, should not cause any pressure and should have sufficient airing slits. The straps must be adjusted exactly and must not hang loosely. Brightly-colored helmets stand out more in traffic. A visor protects one's eyes from dirt and branches.

Illustration 2.5: Only cycle with a helmet! The helmet is just as important as the bike itself

A good helmet is available in several sizes with numerous adjustment possibilities as well as an ingenious ventilation system. The new so-called *Immolding helmets* are the sturdiest and provide more protection than normal hard-top helmets. They are therefore also somewhat more expensive and should not weigh much more than 300g.

For the winter months one can buy thin but warm hats with integrated earwarmers for under the helmet.

Tip

The pads inside the helmet can be taken out and washed gently. The straps should also be cleaned occasionally with soapy water. After a fall on one's head it is imperative that a new helmet be bought.

2.6 Wind Bibs, Leggings & the Rest

The following items of clothing, often with strange names, were specially designed for cyclists and they fulfil those conditions typical for biking.

Gloves

Gloves cushion the hands against the hard handlebars preventing blisters on the palms of one's hands on hard-going trails and to protect them from scrapes and grazes in a fall. In rainy weather, gloves improve one's grip on the handlebars.

When buying, one should ensure that the gloves fit well, as gloves that are too big fall in folds thus causing marks and blisters. Depending on the purpose, long gloves with sewed-on mini-protectorsare also suitable for biking (even in the summer).

Detachables Sleeves and Leggings

Detachable sleeves and leggings can be used between seasons on a cool summer morning or on a cold day. These are cut-off sleeves or trouser legs, which can be pulled on under the tricot or pants. They are available in various materials. Thermo-leggings offer sufficient protection against the cold, right into the late autumn.

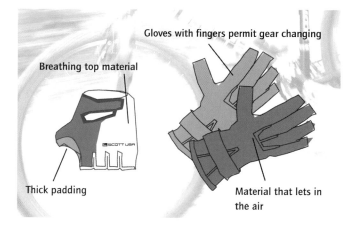

Gloves with fingers permit gear changing

Breathing top material

Thick padding

Material that lets in the air

Illustration 2.6: Gloves cushion the hands against vibrations

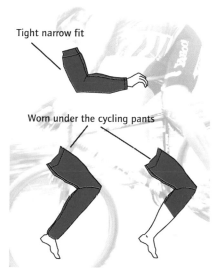

Tight narrow fit

Worn under the cycling pants

*Illustration 2.7:
For anyone training
at temperatures
above 50°F / 10°C
only, leggings will be
sufficient.*

Wind Bib

The wind bib is a sleeveless item of clothing which is worn over the chest and under the tricot as a form of wind protection. The front is made of wind-resistant material, the back should be of thin or netted material.

Waterproof Jacket

Every biker should have a waterproof or weatherproof jacket in his equipment, as they are not only needed for rainy rides or sudden showers, but are also used for long downhill phases or when returning home from a tour in the evening to prevent the biker from losing body heat. The waterproof jacket should have a zip or velcro fastening and the back should be longer than the front to stop splashes getting in. Some top models have a hood in the collar as well as various zips for ventilation purposes. Waterproof jackets of a lesser quality are made of material that is resistant to wind and rain, while more expensive jackets on the other hand are made of fabric that is waterproof but still able to breathe. A simple jacket is generally sufficient.

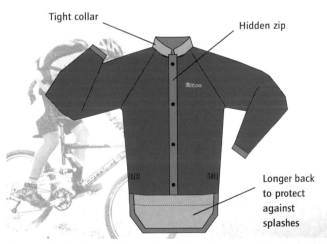

Tight collar

Hidden zip

Longer back to protect against splashes

Illustration 2.8: A waterproof jacket is longer in the back thus preventing the biker's bottom from getting wet, breathable inserts at the side are responsible for ventilation

A 'breathable' waterproof serves well, particularly in bad weather, as it also keeps dirt away from the clothing underneath.

Wind Waistcoat
When no rain is forecasted, it pays off to wear a wind waistcoat (without sleeves), being a very useful item of clothing for descents or during cool times.

Socks
Special short socks are part of the basic equipment. Made out of Coolmax®, they ensure that your feet are dry and at the right temperature. One can identify immediately what kind of cyclist a person is by the socks he's wearing. In racing circles, tennis socks or even knee-length socks are totally frowned upon! Unfortunately however, racing socks are excessively expensive (5-10 $).

Cycling Sunglasses
There are many benefits to one's eyes of wearing sunglasses in training or in competition: at very fast speeds they keep out the strong airstream, they prevent insects and branches from getting in and reduce ultraviolet rays. Apart from tinted sunglasses for sunny weather there are also clear glasses and glasses that even brighten up the surroundings on dull days. Glasses with interchangeable lenses are a good idea.

Illustration 2.9: Cycling glasses should not only look good, they must above all be functional and protect one's eyes

2.7　Winter Clothing

An athlete who trains the whole year around needs not only warm clothing for autumn and spring, but in particular for winter. With the right clothes it is then possible to still go cycling at temperatures below freezing point.

Thermal Pants
At low temperatures a pair of thermal pants protect the muscles and joints from excessive loss of heat. The material is thicker and napped inside thus forming an insulating layer from the wind and the cold outside. Integrated wind protectors for the knee are also recommendable.

Winter Jacket
Modern winter jackets widely surpass their predecessors as far as insulation performance is concerned. They keep you warm so well that one often only needs to wear a functional shirt under a winter jacket made of wind-stopping material. A fleece lining and a high, tight collar ensure a warm body even on cold days. Unfortunately though, these modern winter jackets are not exactly cheap (100-150$).

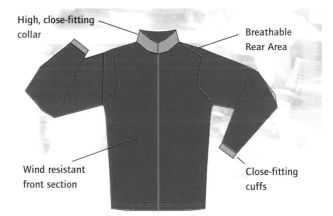

High, close-fitting collar

Breathable Rear Area

Wind resistant front section

Close-fitting cuffs

Illustration 2.10: A winter jacket must have a high warm collar

Overshoes

Overshoes made of neoprene keep cold, wet and any dirt away from one's feet and shoes. As opposed to other materials, neoprene has significant advantages: it's waterproof, it insulates, it has a long life and is easily kept clean. With mountain biking, however, overshoes wear down pretty quickly due to the numerous passages where one has to push the bike along. For this reason one must make sure to have a good, stable sole.

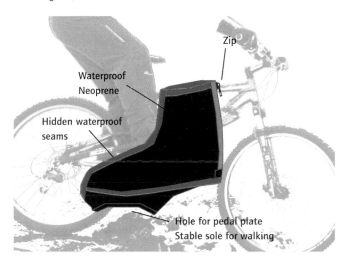

Illustration 2.11: Overshoes made of neoprene keep your feet warm, even in wet weather

To protect one's feet from wet and wind one can additionally wear a freezer bag under one's socks. **Tip**

Thermal Gloves

Thermal gloves are also available in different materials. The important thing is that they are flexible enough to hold onto the handlebars, which is not the case with Alpine skiing gloves for example. Cross-country skiing gloves are perfectly suitable for biking as long as it's not too cold. Gloves with a layer of windstopper material are thin but still very warm.

2.8 Suitable Clothing for all Types of Weather

> 30° C   (Functional undershirt), tricot (long zip), cycling pants,
> 86°F   (cycling socks), helmet.

25-30° C   Functional undershirt, tricot (long zip), cycling pants, cyling
77-86°F   socks, helmet.

20-25° C   Functional undershirt perhaps with windbreaker or wind
68-77°F   bib, tricot, cycling pants, cycling socks, helmet.

15-20° C   Functional undershirt perhaps with windbreaker or wind bib,
59-68°F   jersey with oversleeves or long-sleeved tricot, cycling pants
            with knee/leggings, wind waistcoat, cycling socks, helmet.

10-15° C   Functional undershirt with windbreaker or wind bib, tricot
50-59°F   plus long-sleeved jersey, cycling pants with leggings or long
            pants, wind waistcoat, cycling socks, helmet (long gloves).

5-10° C   Functional undershirt (long-sleeved) with windbreaker or
41-50°F   wind bib, winter jacket and tricot, winter pants, stockings,
            overshoes, helmet, winter gloves.

0-5° C   Functional undershirt (long-sleeved) with windbreaker or
32-41°F   wind bib, winter jacket and polo-neck pullover, over this
            perhaps a windproof jacket, winter pants, warm knee-
            length socks, overshoes, helmet, hat with earwarmers,
            winter gloves.

-5-0° C   Functional undershirt (long-sleeved) with windbreaker or
23-32°F   wind bib, winter jacket and polo-neck pullover and long-
            sleeved tricot, over this perhaps a windproof jacket, winter
            pants, knee-warmers, warm knee-length socks, overshoes,
            helmet, hat with earwarmers, face mask, winter gloves.

< -5° C   See above. Training at these temperatures should last a
< 23°F   maximum of 1.5 hours.

Rain

Experienced bikers are mostly familiar with the weather and only take a waterproof jacket with them when it's likely to rain. Beginners are better taking a waterproof folded up in their tricot pocket with them all the time, as a ride home in the rain for over an hour at temperatures suddenly as low as 50°F/10°C often leads to a feverish cold.

Basic Outfit

For someone who wants to do training mainly in spring and summer as well as on warm days in the autumn will find a basic set containing the following items of clothing sufficient:

Functional undershirt perhaps with a windbreaker (30 $) or wind bib, tricot (45 $), with oversleeves (20 $), cycling pants (50 $) with knee-length socks (20 $) or leggings (20 $), wind waistcoat (30 $), cycling socks (10 $), helmet (60 $).

The prices stated here are a rough guideline as there are huge differences depending on manufacturer and quality. The prices are for products in the middle price level.

For winter temperatures of about 32°F/0°C, one would also need a winter jacket (100$), winter pants (75 $) as well as overshoes (25 $) and gloves (25 $).

3   OPTIMAL SEATING

If you want to be fast, effective and safe on uphills and downhills and wish to avoid having problems on your bike, you have to set and adjust the mountain bike correctly. The next few pages explain just how to do this.

You're best off working in the same order as described here; the seat/top-tube distance for example can only be set when the seat height has already been correctly adjusted beforehand.

Experienced bikers or special cycling stores will all have a variety of tips and formulas for setting positions. For this reason the most important rules are briefly explained here and these will even help inexperienced bikers to set and adjust their mountain bike by themselves.

> Treat the tips recommended here on setting and adjustment as a basis for your own individual fine tuning. The majority of bikers fare very well with these settings and very few of them require an individual solution. **Tip**

3.1   Height of Saddle

You begin adjusting your bike with the saddle height. Select a bike frame that fits in with your own height; a frame that is too big or too small causes problems when being adjusted. When you start off with the right frame size, the height of the saddle needs then only be adjusted by using the saddle binder belt.

Illustration 3.1: Setting/Adjustment of saddle height

A simple method for setting the height of the saddle works well in particularly with the old-fashioned hook pedals, which mountain bikes in the lower price category still quite often have. One sits on the bike and holds onto a wall for support. With the heels placed on the underside of the pedals one pedals backward. The knees should be stretched without the biker having to move around on his saddle. The knees are almost completely straight when doing this.

Tip

This simple method also enables an approximate setting with clipless pedals, however, the position chosen here must be altered again later according to feeling when necessary.

A lower saddle height and the lesser straightening of the knees associated with this, is better for high pedalling frequencies, bike control is also better. A higher saddle position with a low pedalling frequency and a corresponding higher application of pedal force is more adventageous.

Low for Downhills, High for Marathon

A mountainbiker normally sits lower than a racing cyclist in order to have better control over his bike in difficult patches. If you look at the individual MTB disciplines the low saddle heights can be noticed in all the technical disciplines (e.g. downhill, dual slalom, trial). Trial is ridden with an extremely low saddle. Those doing technique training should also lower their saddle. However, more about this in Chapter 4 "Bike Control". Bikers generally sit higher up for cross-country and marathon.

A saddle secured by seat-post quick release is of enormous advantage in biking. Before a difficult single trail downhill, for example, you can quickly lower the saddle for your own safety.

The Formula

Besides the simple method described above, it is also possible to calculate the saddle height using a formula. Before this, you have to determine your inside leg length and this is done by standing against a wall in socks, slightly straddled (5-10cm). With the help of a narrow book pressed (vertically) into the crotch, one makes a mark on the wall, which is then measured. This mark indicates the distance between the floor and the crotch. This value, multiplied by 0.89, gives us the saddle height (centre of pedal bearing-upper edge of saddle).

Despite all formulas and advice on setting the height of a saddle, you must be guided by your own personal feeling when cycling, as no given formula can take individual factors into consideration; for this reason the formula is always to be seen as a rough guide.

New Shoes
When buying new shoes and before attaching a new pedalling system to a bike, it is necessary to measure the current distance between the inner sole of the shoes (over axle) and the upper edge of the saddle (pedals are parallel to saddle tube) in order to be able to set the exact same saddle height for the new shoes or pedals.

Leisure bikers in particular can often be seen cycling with their saddle too low. This hinders the development of the full power of pedalling as well as placing a greater degree of pressure on the kneecaps.

New saddles lose some height after a certain period of use – they wear out – and this means that the saddle height must be readjusted. When a saddle is found to be too low, one should only raise it gradually, about 0.5cm every two weeks in order to prevent any injuries to the joints. Even for 'occasional' cyclists this is the case; one may not adjust the saddle by several centimeters from one day to the next.

3.2   Angle of Saddle

Not only the height but also the angle of the saddle must be adjusted. An MTB saddle is set to a fully horizontal position as this ensures the best possible distribution of pressure, which in turn can also prevent any sores and pressure marks appearing. If the tip of a saddle is pointing downward there is then too much pressure on the arms, besides this one keeps on sliding forward. If the saddle is pointing upward there is no danger any more of one sliding forward, but the urethra and prostate gland are exposed to more pressure instead, and this can cause unpleasant pain.

Illustration 3.2: Adjusting the angle of the saddle

Just as bad is the fact that the pelvis is tilted backward when the saddle is in such a position. There is then more strain on the lumbar spine and this can also lead to pain, in the worst case even to changes of the corpus vertebrae (over a number of years).

Despite these general rules, one also sees experienced bikers cycling with other saddle positions. This again confirms what I said earlier, the adjustments and settings explained here are to be seen as a basis for your own personal fine tuning and which have to be modified to match your own anatomy.

Tip

The best way to adjust a saddle in a horizontal position is with a spirit-level.

3.3   Pedal Adjustment

The next task on the agenda is the adjustment of the tricky pedal plates. In order to prevent any later problems with your knees, feet or hips, this adjustment must be carried out with extreme accuracy. It often happens that, for comfort's sake, bikers continue cycling with a pedal plate that hasn't been adjusted properly and this can lead to the development of overstrained joints (arthrosis) over a period of several years.

If, after setting the pedals, the foot position while pedalling feels any way uncomfortable, they must then be altered again millimeter by millimeter until they fit.

Normally the foot sits in the pedals parallel to the cranks. Only in the case of faulty positions of the joint should one deviate from this rule.

Big Toe over the Axle

The pedal plates are set longwise in such a way that the main joint of the big toe (center of the ball of the foot) is exactly over the middle of the pedal axle; only this enables the effective transmission of the downthrust, because the impulse of force, just as when running, is transferred via the ball of the foot.

There is no adjustment aid here; one can however, feel where the split in the joint is and then push it over toward the middle of the pedal's axle. The feet should be placed wide apart corresponding to the hips. Most pedal systems offer 1-2cm room for adjustment here. Many cyclists try to keep their shoes as close as possible to the cranks without actually touching them with the ankle joints.

Pedal Plate Trick

One normally tightens the plate screws as far as possible when adjusting so that the plates don't twist. This is a very time-consuming procedure and with the following trick it is possible to get the right setting: set the pedal hardness to *hard* and click your foot in to moderately tight plates. Now, with the plate fixed, you are able to move your shoe around until you have found the ideal position.

There are now two possibilities for keeping this position. First of all climb carefully out of your shoes (still in the pedals) without twisting the plates. You can either unscrew the pedal, remove the shoe and tighten the plates properly or mark out the plate's position on the sole of the shoe with a pen and then click out again (plate twists around here). You can now tighten the screws of the plates according to the mark.

Several pedal manufacturers offer good adjustment aids in the form of stencils or brochures, with which an optimal adjustment is possible.

With *Time's* pedalling system you only needs to set the plate's position lengthways. The adjustment at the side is not necessary due to the 5° sideward freedom of movement.

Tip

Tighten the plate screws up well, otherwise you will twist the plate with the sole of your shoe while cycling.

3.4   Saddle Position

Saddle position here refers to the position of the saddle on the saddle-tube; the saddle can move back and forth on its frame by several centimeters. The transmission of power is also optimized by this adjustment.

Knee over Axle

For accurate adjustment you place places the pedal cranks in a horizontal position and then drop a plumb line from the 'back side of the kneecap' (next to the kneecap, about 1cm from the front) through the pedal axle. If the plumb line doesn't touch the pedal axle then the saddle must be moved around until the plumb line is extremely close to the axle at least. Bikers with extremely long or short thighs have to deviate from this position.

Illustration 3.3: The saddle can be moved 4-6cm back and forth depending on model

To adjust the saddle position, with the saddle already parallel to the floor, the cyclist must sit on the bike as normal (your bottom is flush with the rear edge of the saddle). The pedal plates have to be already adjusted beforehand for this setting.

3.5   Handlebar Height

The height of the handlebars is limited by the length of the fork stem and the angle of the front section. The difference in height between the top of the saddle and the top of the handlebars should be a maximum of 6-8cm. Hobby bikers should try to set saddle and handlebars to the same height, this is only possible with a frame of moderate geometric shape.

Illustration 3.4: Adjusting the handlebar height of modern "Ahead" systems is generally only possible with a change of the front fork system

It is often possible to observe differences in height of 10-12cm. Large differences put a lot of strain on the spinal column and can cause changes in the spinal column with young athletes in particular. Lumbar and dorsal vertebral columns are hunched too much and the cervical vertebral column is overstretched due to the low posture. Bikers with very long arms need a larger difference, however.

React to Back Pain
If you feel pain around the area of the lumbar or cervical column the position must be changed. If you already have had problems with your back (e.g. slipped disc) then only the slightest or even no difference is allowed between the height of the saddle and handlebars.

3.6   Seat Distance

The seat distance refers to the distance between the tip of the saddle and the centre of the handlebars. It is determined by the length of the frame's top tube and the saddle position.

Bicycle frames off the peg will have a top tube with a standard length appopriate to the frame height; with 'tailor-made' products one can, within the tight limits allowed, have an influence on the length of the top tube. Most bikers, however, buy a complete bike, where they have little influence on the above-mentioned measurements. For this reason one should consider this criterion when buying a new bike.

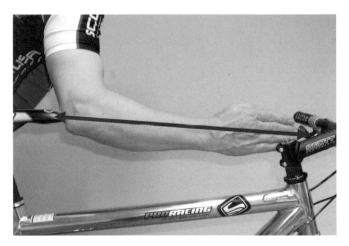

Illustration 3.5: Adjustment of seat distance

The saddle position should not be changed to reset the seat distance where possible, as this has already been individually adjusted to suit the length of your thighs. So only the length of the front section remains to be able to alter the seat distance. The right feeling plays an important role when doing this adjustment, because what counts in the end is that you feel comfortable sitting on the mountain bike.

The position must neither be too oustretched and flat, nor too upright. It must be possible also to cycle long stretches with the handlebars in this position without your back complaining. For bikers who are overweight, this position is also a problem, so finding the optimal solution here is of utmost importance.

When all settings on the bike are completed you will find the position at first extremely uncomfortable and very stretched. This disappears during the first 1,000km as your body gets accustomed to this new situation very quickly.

3.7   Length of Crank

Mountain bikes are generally only built with cranks 175mm long, which because of their length ensure good forward drive on steep hills. However, cyclists who are shorter than 165cm should think about cycling with shorter pedal cranks that are 170mm in length. 175mm cranks can cause problems for those with very short legs. These come in the form of knee troubles due to the strong flexing movements. The short pedal crank enables a higher pedal frequency, whereas the long crank ensures better transmission of power (longer lever arm), but this of course is at the expense of a lower pedalling frequency and curve angle.

3.8   Measurement Record

When you have found your ideal position it's worth starting a measurement record containing all the relevant adjustment measurements. This enables quick adjustment of a new bike. The following data should be included:

1. Frame height (center of pedal bearing-top of saddle tube)
2. Seat height (center of pedal bearing-top of saddle).
3. Frame length (center of handlebar tube of saddle tube).
4. Seat distance (tip of saddle to center of handlebars).
5. Length of front protusion of the handlebars (from imbus point to forward throw of handlebar).
6. Saddle depth.
7. Longitudinal distance between center of pedal bearing and forward point of saddle.
8. Length of crank (center of pedal bearing-center of pedal axle).

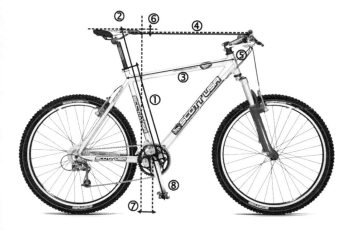

1 _____

2 _____

3 _____

4 _____

5 _____

6 _____

Illustration 3.6:
You can enter your individual   7 _____
measurements here

8 _____

4 BIKE CONTROL – THE OPTIMAL BIKING TECHNIQUE

The following chapter explains the basic biking techniques. Important here is the great number of tips based on practical experience. Many exercises help you to improve your biking technique efficiently. Even professional bikers carry out regular technique training in order to be faster in competition.

However, remember that complex techniques such as the *Bunny Hop* cannot be learned overnight. Even the real biking freaks need weeks or even months to manage difficult tricks like the *Nose Wheelie* (balancing on the front wheel). So be patient, and your technique will improve a little bit each time.

Stay with It
Practice makes perfect, and at some stage or other it will click and you can suddenly manage for example balancing, standing still on the bike. Include a few minutes of technique training in every session you do. What's wrong with a bit of hopping and balancing while waiting for a friend or standing at the traffic lights. Make use of these opportunities!

Clipless Pedals
If you already have clipless pedals, you should get familiar with the engaging and disengaging procedure before all other exercises, as there is nothing more embarrassing than a fall with your shoes still locked in position. Not only that, one can end up with serious fractures of the arm and shoulder after such a fall. This position can be unlocked by simply twisting one's foot inward or outward.

4.1 Gear Changing

The new gear systems enable incredibly pleasant gear changing with up to 27 gears. Deciding when to change gear is still left to the cyclist's own discretion.

Brief Relief

So not to overtax the gear rim and cog wheel too much, you should ease pedal pressure slightly before changing gear. Even modern gear shifts don't work well at low pedal frequency, so don't forget to keep pedalling (a common beginner's mistake). Changing gears on a hill under load is something, which you must practice in particular. Only the real pros can manage to shift gears here without any grinding and creaking because they drop off pedal pressure. One should change gears gradually and not skip over many gears at one go.

Changing a Gear Early Enough

One should change gears according to the situation and particularly in good time i.e. before a tight curve, a narrow trail or an uphill patch.

Because of the high loss of friction and increased wear and tear, you should not cycle with a crooked chain line e.g. large disc at the front with the largest gear at the back or small disc and smallest gear.

The Right Ratio

Choosing the right gear ratio depends a lot on the particular situation and is mostly determined by pedalling frequency. The choice of ratio serves to adapt individual performance capacity to the going, the situation and the type of surface underneath. Pedalling frequency should be approximately 90 revolutions/minute both in competition and in training (except for certain forms of training). It must sometimes be higher in training.

A common mistake made by beginners is to use an excessively high gear ratio. They then train the whole time with the large disc, which not only considerably reduces the training effect, but also involves a significantly higher amount of strain on the locomotor system.

Exercises
1) Change through all gears (front and rear) except for those mentioned above and get a feeling for the various ratios.
2) Ease off briefly on a hill, change gear and then raise pedalling pressure again (front and rear).
3) Stop and Go: Before coming to a stop change into an easy gear and when setting off again move up a gear again according to speed.

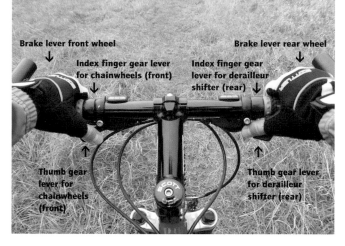

Illustration 4.1: Biker's cockpit. Each lever has a different function

4.2 Braking

Braking is an absolute elementary technique of biking beacause, as opposed to cycle racing, one has to brake very often and sometimes very abruptly.

Front Brake Is More Important than the Rear Brake

The front and rear brakes work at differing strengths: two thirds of one's braking force is achieved with the front brake and about a third by the rear brake. Due to the weaker road grip and the shift of weight toward the front, the rear wheel locks much faster than the front wheel.

What one has to learn then, is how to apply the brakes in such a way that the wheels don't lock and the bike doesn't skid or throw the biker over the handlebars. Obviously one has to know first where the front brake is, and on most bikes it's usually on the left.

What makes the correct brake dosage in biking difficult is the frequent changes in the surface underneath. Only with a lot of experience is a correct estimation of the various surfaces possible.

Always Brake with Both Brakes

A biker basically uses both brakes when braking and strives to achieve a brake maneuver with the correct dosage measurement. In the case of a full slam on of the brakes, strong braking before a curve or going downhill, your body weight is shifted to the back by stretching your arms and pushing the posterior right back over the the saddle. With this technique you are basically standing in the pedals, which are both at the same height.

Illustration 4.2: Standing brake position

 Be Careful: The brake effect on wet wheel rims is not as good as on dry rims.

Exercises

1) Gradually get used to the brakes on a route or on an area and increase speed until you slam on the brakes. Don't let the front or rear wheel lock, by any means.

2) Carry out slamming on the brakes at a marked point in the standing brake position without the wheels locking.

3) Carry out braking maneuvers with the rear wheel locking. Later on, practice sliding on the locked rear wheel.

4) By applying the front brake briefly but strongly and then letting go again immediately let the front wheel lock briefly on slippy surfaces.

4.3 Uphill

A special technique is required when cycling uphill on a mountain bike in order to ensure as an effficient a climb as possible. You can separate the wheat from the chaff on short, steep climbs, as an advanced biker can cycle up very steep ramps, whereas the beginner has to get off his bike immediately. It is not physical condition, but rather the biking technique that limits the beginner's ability on short climbs.

Compact Uphill Cycling

The steeper the hill the smaller a biker has to make himself in order to prevent the front wheel from lifting or the rear wheel from spinning. You slide forward on the saddle and tuck yourself in – you are almost biting into the handlebars. This means that both wheels are equally loaded.

You change into the right gear early enough in order to be able to pedal fluently at a high frequency. With a heavier gear the pedalling frequency drops too dramatically and you end up standing still. When the ascent is very steep you have to expect to come to a standstill and for this reason one must be able to master the skill of getting out of the pedals quickly.

The rocking position takes too much weight off the rear wheel and this causes it to spin. If you really want to cycle in the rocking position then it is necessary to transfer your weight to the rear.

Illustration 4.3: Compact position for steep climbs

Long and Easy Uphill

For long uphill sections which are not too steep you can cycle in a relaxed sitting position with the hands wide apart on the handlebars and the back and shoulder area nice and relaxed, as this hinders breathing to a minimal extent. The best thing is to alternate regularly between sitting position and rocking position so as to put demand on various different groups of muscles. Holding the *'horns'* is an optimal position for rocking.

You should cycle up the flatter uphill sections at a steady speed mainly in a sitting position as more energy is used up in the rocking position than when sitting. The fluent, high-frequenced style with low gear ratio is mostly more economical than the exhausting stamping style with a high level of gear ratio.

Slow and then Full Boost

Several uphill sections tire a biker out because of the various different levels of steepness and ground surfaces. A beginner is particularly somewhat overtaxed here, especially when a ten-minute steep climb is then suddenly followed by a tricky section. For this reason you should cycle up long ascents as slowly as possible in order to have some reserves left over for difficult trails ahead. In the end it should be every biker's aim to be able to manage to cycle for as long as possible up the hill.

Exercises
1) Look for short, steep hills (10-20m) to practice on and then try out various positions (sitting and rocking position with weight transfer).
2) Practice changing gears early enough.
3) Practice the various techniques on long changeable hills.
4) Cycle up technically tricky mountains as slowly as possible, stopping and holding one's balance briefly if need be.

4.4   Downhill

Cycling downhill on the bike offers the ultimate kick and is just as much fun as on skis or on a snowboard. However, many bikers overestimate themselves and expose themselves to unnecessary dangers.

Get up – Stand up!
When cycling downhill over cross-country, you assume the standing position explained above for braking maneuvers in order to be able to use both arms and legs as shock absorbers. The saddle is between the inner thighs, feet are at equal height, your bottom is pushed backward and two fingers are on the brake levers on each side.

Only on very good forest paths or asphalt is it possible to stay sitting and assume a favorable aerodynamic position in order to reach the valley with as little wind resistance as possible.

The speed downhill is normally so high that pedalling is neither necessary nor possible any more. In order for the legs to be able to recover somewhat, one should pedal lightly at suitable stages, shake out the muscles and stretch a little.

Don't Be Afraid of the Drop-in
The **drop-in** normally refers to an almost vertical passage at the beginning of a downhill. Such steep initial sections, however, demand a lot of overcoming for a beginner. If the run out is free then you only needs to push the bike extremely far forward (bottom way behind the

Illustration 4.4: One has to master the downhill position

saddle) and then let the wheels roll. One doesn't start braking until the bike has reached the 'normal' downhill section. If one brakes during the steep section there is a risk of the bike somersaulting. A saddle set to a low position also helps toward better control of the bike.

You cycle the same way on downhills with large terraces, for example through roots and stones, and lets the bike roll for a brief moment. When a biker has once managed to surmount a passage then he'll be able to cycle through it immediately the next time. You just have to overcome your fear on the first attempt. An experienced biker will be of assistance by showing how the passage can be managed without any problems, and by offering some useful advice.

Braking Feeling
On downhills, the fingers are always placed on the brake levers and you brake evenly, not abruptly, with both brakes. The brakes must be set in such a way that the point of pressure (when the wheels lock) lies at about the middle of the lever movement toward the handlebars.

Long Downhills
On long downhill sections, it is best to change between the standing and sitting position on the bike. The hands should also be shaken out alternately on the flutter sections in to avoid cramps.

Exercises
1) The extreme downhill position, with the bottom right behind the saddle is adapted on a flat surface and then released again.
2) On a downhill trail, come from a quick ride to a standstill and then head off again.
3) Practice the downhill position on a short row of steps (3-5) thus also indirectly practicing the **drop-in**.

4.5   Curve Technique

High speed in curves is a fantastic feeling, but if the bike skids it often comes to falls. Beginners must gradually and carefully work up to higher speeds in bends but should not try to keep up with the professionals.

Control Is Everything

First of all before a curve you must reduce speed enough so that you don't skid; experience will tell just how much this speed is. The braking maneuver (both brakes) should always be completed before the curve so that only minor braking corrections are necessary in the curve itself.

One either stands in the pedals (downhill) or remains sitting down, but in any case the arms are bent and the upper body is flat as this lowers your center of gravity and increases stability.

You must change down gear before the curve as well, so that you can start pedalling again after the curve as appropriate.

The Technique

The higher the speed in the curve, the more the leaning-over position of both biker and bike. You should be in line with the bike here. Knees are close to the frame. The knee on the inside of the curve can, in an emergency situation, be bent in order to bring more weight toward the turning point without having having to lay into the curve even further. The pedal on the inside is brought into upper position to avoid it hitting the ground. The outer, outstretched leg is pushed down on to the pedal. More weight is placed on the front wheel when the biker's upper body is in a flat position. The curve is ridden according to the so-called *ideal line*, i.e. you approach it on the far outside, cut into the curve toward the apex and then continue again on the far outside.

By cutting the curve you increase the curve radius from a physics point of view, and reduce centrifugal force in the process. This technique is obviously forbidden in road traffic and should only be used over cross-country on curves you can see into.

Press the Bike!

This describes the technique of *pressing* the bike into the curve on narrow bends that aren't too fast. The bike assumes a more leaning over position than the biker.

Drifting

With the technique described above the biker tries as much as possible not to skid. Drifting on the other hand is when one deliberately makes

Illustration 4.5: Through the curve quickly and safely

controlled skids with the rear wheel. This technique is used mostly on loose ground surfaces as these enable controlled drifting.

Exercises
1) Practice cycling through curves on asphalt first and then on gravelled routes.
2) Press the bike further into the curve than your own body.
3) Set up an uneven slalom and take on the curves with increasing speed.
4) Practice controlled drifting in curves on sandy surfaces.

4.6 Balance

A very good sense of balance is one of the basic skills that a biker should possess. A biker's ability to keep the bike balanced, even on a narrow track and at slow speed levels on all difficult trail passages, is what makes the surmounting of this type of going at all possible. There are many exercises for improving the balance; your own personal creativity is what's asked for here so that you can come to a stop at any random point and keep your balance.

The Technique
It's best to stand in the pedals and then twist the handlebars to the side where the pedal is at the front. The best place for practicing balancing on the spot is on a very slight upward slope as one rolls forward a little (5cm) by applying light pressure on the front pedal, and rolls back again because of the slope and the reduction in pedal pressure. The biker is in a dynamic position of balance with this almost invisible to-and-fro movement, and this is very steady indeed.

Exercises
1) Lean against a wall, then move away from the wall and try to stay standing.
2) Come to a stop and hold your balance, ride on immediately when the bike starts to tip over.
3) Cycle slowly and with the front wheel briefly leaning against a tree, a wall etc, try balancing, then release and cycle on further.
4) Practice a dynamic balanced position as described above.

4.7   Overcoming Obstacles

When cycling on trails and paths, certain obstacles such as holes, rises, stones, branches, roots or kerbs can make it difficult for a biker to get through safely. With a bit of practice it is possible to jump over most of these obstacles or skilfully take the weight off the bike so that the bike doesn't get damaged or the biker fall over.

The Hop Technique
With *the hop,* you jump up with both wheels at the same time and land in this position again. To do this you bring the pedal cranks firstly into a horizontal position and take hold of either the handles or the horns. To begin the movement, you get up out of the saddle and then shift your weight down explosively (flatten yourself, bend elbows and knees). After this, you pull the bike up by the handlebars and pedal as evenly as possible by raising your upper body and pulling your feet up (straighten the knees) without jerking the handlebars.

The pressure on the tires and suspension fork help here. When landing, one gives way with the body, flexing the joints in order to absorb the impact.

Illustration 4.6: Jumping is one of the more complex biking techniques

The Jump Technique

To learn this technique you start off raising either only the front wheel or only the rear wheel. With more and more practice you can then combine both movements into the jump.

Wedge Your Feet

An athlete without clipless pedals must wedge both feet tightly onto the pedals. The tips of your toes point downward and you press backward onto the pedal. At the same time the hands press against the handlebars thus tensing yourself on the bike.

If you wish to jump over an obstacle then you have to approach the obstacle at quite a high speed in order to be able to lift off high enough and in particular far enough.

High obstacles or edges are surmounted slowly with the front wheel lifted up and then with the rear wheel pulled up afterward. Drainage channels or rails should be crossed over in as vertical a position as possible, but never at an acute angle.

Exercises

1) Place weight on the bike and then ease off: as described above, you try to compress the tires and the fork and then ease off again.

2) Pull up the front wheel on its own.

3) Lift up the rear wheel on its own (wedged feet).

4) Surmount branches by lifting one wheel after the other.

5) Lift both wheels simultaneously, following up with a jump.

4.8 Some Little Tricks

As already mentioned, acrobatic tricks are the result of long and intensive training. Anyone who believes he'll be able to hop on the spot after just one day is either a natural prodigy or simply a show-off. It's even more difficult to learn what appear to be easy tricks such as the *nose wheelie* (balancing on the front wheel) or jumping on the rear wheel. Only a biker who is always motivated to practice certain trick elements for a few minutes on every bike tour will actually learn the art of these bike tricks. One can make great use of these on cross-country tours and they also offer an extra portion of safety in certain hair-raising situations.

4.9 Rounded Pedalling

Rounded pedalling can be defined as the steady, even amount of force placed on the pedals throughout an entire pedalling

cycle. However, this is only the theoretical explanation. In practice, however, round pedalling is what distinguishes a racer from a hobby biker, as the many kilometers that a racer has already completed have given him the optimal movement and enable him to carry out this movement in a significantly more economic way. The fixed foot of the racing pedal not only makes treading, i.e. an up and down movement possible, but also a pushing, pressing and pulling movement; an occasional biker on a normal pushbike is not capable of doing this with normal pedals.

Optimal pedalling does not involve just treading downward but also actively pulling the leg up to the rear. One is generally only able to actively overcome the weight of the leg; an additional pulling is only possible when starting off and sprinting.

Tip

In order to learn a pedalling technique, which is as economical as possible, you should train in low gears and at high pedalling frequencies. The odd training session on a hill with higher gears helps you get a feeling for the various movement phases, thus enabling a more successful learning process.

5 FIT WITH THE BIKE – TRAINING FOR BEGINNERS

5.1 From Beginner to Professional!

You have chosen mountain biking to improve your level of fitness. This was the right decision as you can pace out your training in optimal doses, you have a lot of fun on difficult passages and are out enjoying the open countryside. On the next few pages you can find out the best way to train to become fit and healthy. I would recommend anyone wishing to find out more information on racing training in particular to read the book "Mountain Bike Training" (Meyer & Meyer Sport).

Our Body Changes

When a person with little endurance training starts out biking, numerous changes are put into action within his body, which make the organism adapt to the higher performance demands. Apart from visible signs such as a better muscular appearance or loss in weight, further adaptations also take place which are outwardly invisible.

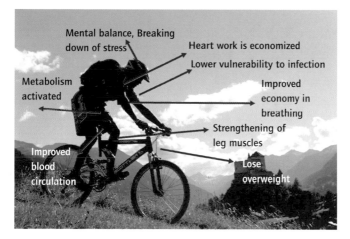

Illustration 5.1: Biking makes you fit and healthy

If you want to compare yourself with experienced bikers, you should always remember that they have become physically adapted to the demands through years of training, and for this reason are generally head and shoulders above you in performance. You have to have a little patience.

5.2   Some Theory as well, Please! Training Principles

Many bikers just head off on their bikes, taking the same route at the same speed each time. Their form is subject only to very slight fluctuations. There are no improvements in performance. Someone who trains according to a system, however, will notice that significant improvements in performance are possible even for hobby bikers. This implies, however, structuring training to certain rules.

Training can thus be defined as a planned process, which aims at maintaining or achieving an improvement in physical performance capacity. From a biological aspect, training denotes the body's reaction to loads. When demands are made of the human body, its physical abilities develop further. When the body is no longer exposed to strain, these abilities diminish again.

Load and Recovery

A sensible combination of load and recovery (rest period) determines the efficiency of training. Strain upsets the body's biological balance with the result that after a recovery phase (**regeneration**), your body adapts itself to the level of load and possesses a higher performance than before.

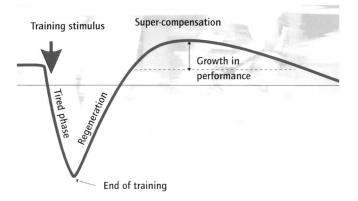

Illustration 5.2: Super-compensation, the fundamental principle for effective training or improvement in performance

What appears to be quite easy in theory or in the illustration is in reality, however, much more complex. If you continue to pursue the idea behind super-compensation then an 'endless' growth in performance should be possible. Super-compensation is actually particularly noticeable among beginners. An improvement in performance can be noted after almost every training session. Once your training state has reached a high level, however, the 'leaps' in performance become much less spectacular, until at the end a solid base of consistent performance capacity exists.

Train with Patience

Because of this fact, highly-trained professional bikers have to carry out very high training volumes according to well thought out training schedules, if they want to retain their performance ability or improve it even more. As a beginner, however, there is no need to worry about this.

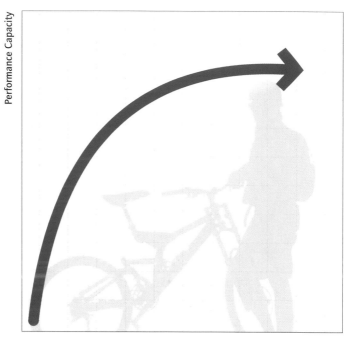

Illustration 5.3: Performance development from long term endurance training with increasing load (schematically shown)

The started graph in 5.4 indicates that the loading of strain is too short; the new stimulus is already started in the regeneration period so that performance capacity cannot grow but drops instead.

A stagnation in performance occurs as a result of insufficient load stimulus; the next load stimulus will only occur when super-compensation has returned again and encounters almost the identical conditions as before training. One achieves little or no growth in performance here.

The lower drawing in 5.4 indicates that the new load must lie within the medium range (climax) of the super-compensation phase, in order to ensure an optimal improvement in performance. Not only the

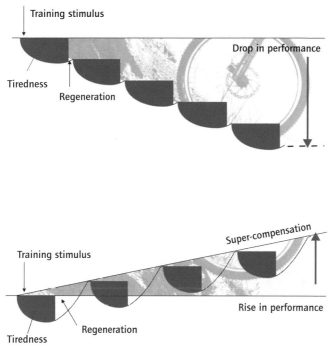

Illustration 5.4: The correct and incorrect stringing together of load stimulus

duration of the regeneration periods between training sessions must be correctly selected; the training load itself must be right, if performance is to grow. A stimulus that is too low will not trigger off any adaptation process – a stimulus that is too high will lead to a state of overtraining in the long term; only the correct stimulus will result in the desired adaption process and super-compensation.

Optimal Training

When choosing recovery phases or setting up training plans, the feeling in your own body plays a significant role. For this reason you must not see a training plan as a rigid structure. You have to modify the plan to fit in with your own physical feeling and individual situation.

In order to ensure that your training is successful, you should pay attention to the general piece of advice below.

Tip

> Bike training must be carried out at least 3x a week for a minimum of 60 minutes load, if one wishes to see clear health benefits and an improvement in performance. Even better would be four training sessions with a total load duration of six hours. The remaining three days in the week are days of rest.

Many bikers often go training two or three days in a row, in order to tire out their body even more; a day of rest doesn't come until later.

Start off Slowly!
Absolute beginners should start out gently and go biking only 1-2x a week at the beginning. Only when you begin to feel fitter, should you increase load.

Description of Training
A training session is characterized by its intensity and volume levels. Intensity refers to how high the load is. The easiest way of finding out training intensity in cycling is by using your heart rate (high intensity = high heart rate).

More about this later. Training volume in cycling sport means the number of kilometers covered or the duration of training (e.g. 12 hours/week).

These terms are used again later on for the training suggestions.

5.3 Regeneration

If one could be successful through hard and tiring daily training alone, then a good number of endurance athletes would have a much higher performance capacity. However, apart from the necessary training loads, a well-structured training program must also include recovery or regeneration. After every hard training session your body must be allowed a rest.

Regeneration Accelerators

- Sufficient Rest (sleep)
- Balanced diet, rich in carbohydrates
- Stretching
- Massage
- Warm bath, shower
- Sauna
- Active recovery (walks)
- Regenerative training.

5.4 How Do I Train?

Intervals and Other Methods

There are various training methods for cycling sport. Depending on the method used you cycle at steady speeds or build certain tempo phases into training. Before learning more about the time sequence in training, here are a few more basic terms.

Continuous Method

With a constant intensity level, load is controlled via the heart rate. The continuous training method is the main method of training in cycling sport, particularly in the preparation period, as it improves endurance capacity (aerobic) and regeneration ability. Load duration should be over an hour and can go on for up to five hours.

Speed Games/Fartlek

Speed is adapted according to terrain and the prevailing wind conditions. The biker plays with speed and thus with intensity. Fartlek is particularly carried out on rough surfaces. The intensity is considerably limited however.

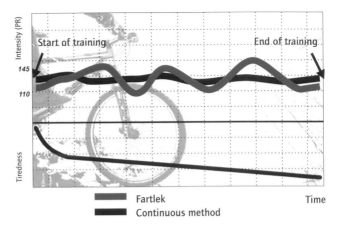

Illustration 5.5: Continuous method vs. fartlek

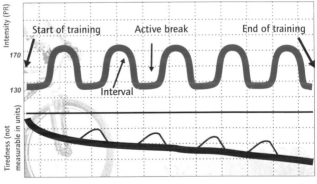

Illustration 5.6: Interval method

The interval method can be characterized by the planned changeover from load to recovery; the recovery interval is not long enough for complete recovery; a new load interval begins again when the heart rate lies between 120-140. In the case of short load intervals (6-40 sec) the break lasts for about 1-2 minutes, for longer load intervals of 60 sec – 10 min the break goes on for 5 – 20 min depending on performance capacity. During the breaks you continue cycling in a low gear.

How Do I Train? Training Intensities

In order to achieve an improved structure in training you divide it up according to training intensities, which correspond to various areas of metabolism. More information on training areas are listed in the tables below.

Compensatory Training (CO)

Compensation means balancing something out and compensatory training involves balancing out a load or tiredness. The aim is reached through active recovery appropriate to the type of sport. Compensatory training should take place when your body is in a very exhausted state. It has the lowest training intensity of all training levels and reaches a low area of aerobic metabolism.

Compensatory Training – CO

Description:	Regenerative training in order to work on performance capacity following intensive loads in training and competition, or for warming up before loads.
Heart rate:	80-120 bpm.
Distance/Going:	10-30km, flat.
Pedalling rate:	70-100 rpm.
Gear ratio:	4.60-6.00m.
	42 x 20-16.
Method:	Continuous method.
Form of organization:	Individual and group training.
Tips:	Exert as little pressure as possible on the pedals, be warmly dressed, technique training can also be incorporated into compensatory training; very important in training camps.

Illustration 5.7: Compensatory Training

Basic Endurance Training 1 (BE 1)

The most important training intensity in biking occurs in Basic Endurance Training 1, which works on aerobic metabolism. This is a training intensity at which fat burning occurs excellently and is therefore, from a health aspect (overweight), the most favorable of all. A competitive biker carries out a very high percentage (75%) of his entire training for the whole year within this region. Only when basic endurance has reached a high level is it possible to cope with high loads under anaerobic conditions such as steep hills for example.

Basic Endurance 1 training sessions can be characterized by large to very large training volumes at low intensity and are preferably carried out on roads.

Basic Endurance Training 1 – BE1

Description:	Most important training area for mountain bikers, for warming up before load.
Heart rate:	115-145 bpm.
Distance/Going:	50 – 150km, flat to bumpy.
Duration:	2:00 – 5:00 hours.
Pedalling rate:	80-110 rpm, optimal 100 rpm.
Gear ratio:	4.70 – 6.40m e.g. 42 x 19-14
Method:	Continuous method.
Form of organization:	Individual training is the most favorable form here, intensity control via heart rate.
Group training:	Frequent change in group leader in order to keep intensity steady (1-2 min).
Tips:	Try not to train above a heart rate of 150 bpm where possible, fluctuation range of about 20 beats is optimal, speed is not an important parameter.

Illustration 5.8: Basic Endurance Training 1 (BE 1)

Basic Endurance Training 2 (BE 2)

The BE 2 area works on the lower region of the aerobic/anaerobic threshold. The following paragraph deals with individual heart rate in the various training intensities. What makes sense is to include a few BE 2 intervals into a BE 1 training session. A long training tour (over 2 hours), which is carried out exclusively in the BE 2 area, leads to extreme tiredness and should seldom be incorporated into your training plan.

Basic Endurance 2 – BE 2

Description:	Training at moderate intensity.
Heart rate:	approx. 145-165 bpm.
Distance/Going:	5-70km, flat to bumpy.
Duration:	0:15 – 2:00 h.
Pedalling rate:	80-120 rpm.
Gear ratio:	5.60 – 7-60m. e.g. 42 x 16-52 x 15.
Method:	Repetition method.
Form of organization:	Individual training: self-motivation not easy, intensity control via heart rate and pedalling frequency;
Group training:	Frequent change of group leader to keep intensity steady (1-2 min).
Tips:	Fluctuation range of about 10-15 beats is optimal, speed is not a parameter of control; distance refers to entire BE 2 distance.

Illustration 5.9: BE 2

Race Specific Endurance (RSE)

Training within the RSE area is orientated toward competition speed and competition load and is therefore allocated to the upper range of the aerobic/anaerobic threshold and anaerobic area. This form of training can be carried out excellently on cross-country with the MTB.

Race Specific Endurance – RSE

Description:	Training at high intensity for improving stamina, training of speed sensation.

Heart rate:	Approx. 160 – 185 bpm.
Distance/Going:	10-50km; flat to hilly.
Duration:	0:20 – 1:30 h.
Pedalling rate:	80 – 120 rpm, optimal is 100 rpm.
Gear ratio:	6.20-9.20m
	e.g. 52 x 18-52 x 12.
Method:	Repetition method, competition method
Form of organization:	Individual training: timed training, intensity control via heart rate.
Group training:	team timed training.

Tips:	Range of fluctuation of about 20 beats is optimal, speed is not a parameter of control, race rehearsal.

Illustration 5.10: RSE

How Do I Train? Training which Is Oriented toward Heart Rates

If you just want to check your training intensity when biking, then it is worth investing in a heart rate monitor. It is then possible to calculate your individual training intensities by using simple formulas. Heart rate monitors are available for from 50 $ upward.

Heart Rate Behavior when Biking

Heart rates while biking (unlike running) are prone to relatively large fluctuations, depending on the going and weather. However, finding the desired intensity level is no problem when one brings the right gear and pedalling frequency into line. What's of prior importance here is no longer the constant speed, but rather the heart rate. It is considerably more difficult though to keep the intensity levels steady on cross-country.

Illustration 5.11: Operating a heart rate monitor is child's play

How Does a Heart Rate Monitor Help?
Intensities too high

An inevitable consequence of pulse-oriented training is for example that one has to cycle more slowly with a headwind or uphill in order not to exceed the level of intensity desired (e.g. BE 1).

Intensities too low

Certain training intensities and methods must be carried out at very high or the highest intensities, and this is very difficult to estimate without a heart rate monitor. With a bit of experience it is also possible to assess your current form from the heart rate. To do this you have to carefully observe your pulse under various forms of load and at rest.

Rest Pulse

The rest pulse is measured in bed before getting up in the morning and can often indicate the arrival of illnesses before the symptoms appear. If the pulse at rest rises gradually over a number of days this normally indicates a regeneration deficit.

In the case of an upward difference of 6-8 beats per minute one should check the above factors and be careful with your load intensity in training and competition, particularly when your heart rate is also higher than normal; where necessary one should even stop cycling altogether. Endurance training when suffering from infection or illness can lead to damage of the heart muscle and other organs.

Maximal Heart Rate

Maximal heart rate is only reached under the highest load level and can be different for the same person for various types of sport.
Anyone who is in good physical health and has had this confirmed by his GP can test his maximal heart rate with a heart rate monitor.

After a warm-up program of 30 minutes, you should cycle at maximum speed for 3-4 minutes (best slightly uphill) and then read the heart rate showing after stopping. There is, however, a formula with which you can roughly calculate your maximal pulse. However, it is a 'rough' calculation, as there are sometimes significant deviations from this rate.

220 – age = maximal heart rate (MHR)
(230 for women)

Calculating the Areas of Intensity

To calculate your heart rate under load, you take the rest pulse, the maximal heart rate as well as the factor of intensity.

Step 1:	Subtract rest pulse from MHR	
Step 2:	Multiply this rate by the intensity factor	
Step 3:	Rest pulse is added to this rate again	
Example:	Step 1:	$200 - 50 = 150$
	Step 2:	$150 \times 0.65 = 97$
	Step 3:	$97 + 50 = 147$

The rate calculated here would be the upper pulse limit for Basic Endurance Training 1 (BE 1) for the person in question.

Factors of Intensity

Training Intensities	Factor
Compensatory Area – CO	up to 0.52
Basic Area 1 – BE 1	0.52 – 0.65
Basic Area 2 – BE 2	0.65 – 0.82
Race Specific Endurance – RSE	0.75 – 0.95

These factors give the lower and upper limits of the area in question.

You can enter your training heart rates into the following table:

	Rest pulse		Maximal pulse	
CO	from		to	
BE 1	from		to	
BE 2	from		to	
RSE	from		to	

5.5 When Do I Train? Dividing up the Training Year into Periods

With knowledge of training intensities and training methods alone it may be possible to head off with training straight away, but just how successful you are is a matter of coincidence. For this reason you have to bring a structure into training and this is done by dividing the training year up into phases. In the preparation phase you lay the foundation for the oncoming competition phase where a long tour or a crossing of the Alps has been planned for example. Less training is done in the transitional phase and your performance capacity drops again.

The aim of such a year's division is to bring out your best possible form (according to time factors and other situations).

Training Plans
The individual training periods are illustrated below with a sample weekly training plan in each case. These sample weekly training plans are only a suggestion for training in a particular period. When setting up your own training plan you should stick to the advice given in "Training Errors" and proceed strictly according to the 2:1 or 3:1 principle, which is explained below.

When planning the year, you're best working according to the following scheme.

1. Setting Aims
You enter your aims for the coming year (tours, cycling holiday, marathon; no more than two or three) in a calendar that is clearly laid out.

2. Transitional Period
Enter in the transitional period (autumn) where you would only like to do a little training. Duration: 3-5 weeks.

3. Preparation Period
Plan the months of preparation up to your first real aim for the year. The 2:1 or 3:1 principle (for weeks) is very important here. Duration: at least 12 weeks up to your first aim, and then considerably shorter.

4. Week of Rest
A recovery phase takes place after the first event.

5. Remaining Aims for the Year
Prepare for all other aims in exactly the same way as under 3.

Working without a Training Plan
It is obviously possible to train without any particular aims for the season. In order to prevent possible overtraining, you should, however, orientate yourself to basic training principles. In order to stay fit and healthy, you should carry out training at least 3x a week for over 60 minutes at basic intensity.

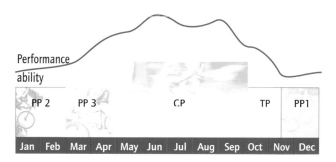

Illustration 5.12: Clear overview of the periods in the year

Preparation Period
The preparation period lasts from November or December until about April. Throughout this time and particularly in the winter months, you should also carry out other types of sport where at all possible. Training intensities are low, intensive training sessions should be measured out in doses carefully, but needn't be left out altogether. The aim here is to improve your basic endurance.

Cross-training
An excellent method for improving your basic endurance is cross-training. Cross-training implies carrying out several different types of endurance sports. Particularly suitable for cross-training are the following types of sport:

Illustration 5.13: Cross-training offers a good deal of variety

Inline skating, cross-country skiing, roller skiing, agua-jogging, swimming, aerobics, running, walking, hill-climbing and other forms of endurance sports.

Advantages of Cross-training

- Improves movement experience and your personal physical feeling.
- Acquires new reserves of performance.
- Mental balance.
- Active recovery.
- Prevention of overstraining in one particular area.

Competition/Marathon Period

The competition period runs from about May to October. For the ambitious hobby sportsman it would be better to change it to 'nice weather period' or 'marathon period'. Load is increased in the competition period, either continually up to the highlight of the season or with an interim highlight. This increase in load is stopped two weeks before the seasonal highlight, however. After that you only carry out a small amount of easy training.

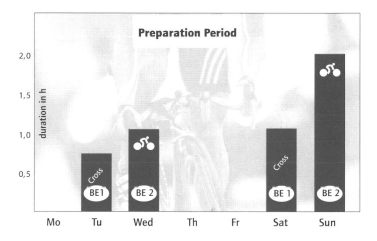

Illustration 5.14: Sample plan for the Preparation Period

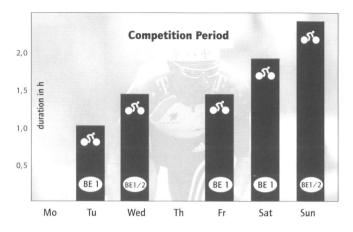

Illustration 5.15: Sample plan for the Competition Period

Transitional Period
The transitional period from October to November is a period of regeneration from everyday training or competition. For medical reasons one should keep up with exercise and not give up training completely.

One should only refrain from cycling in this phase in order to tank up with motivation for the oncoming preparation periods. The transitional period generally lasts for 3-5 weeks.

2:1 or 3:1
2:1 is not a football score but rather a load-recovery cycle. The training plans are set up according to the important principle of periods and cycles. Two or three weeks with increasing load are always followed by a week of rest with less training.

You use exactly the same structure for the week; a day of rest comes after two or three days of training. This so-called **2:1** or **3:1 cycle** has made its mark in the area of endurance sports. With this rhythm your body can adapt itself to the loads in the optimal way and is not overworked.

5.6   Training Errors

- Too intensive training, which takes place mainly within the BE 2 and CO areas.

- When training has been too intensive during the week, it is not possible to bring out your best performance on a long tour or marathon at the weekend. A poor state of regeneration (constant exhaustion) and empty glycogen stores are a characteristic feature here.

- Underestimation of your work load, which in the case of training not being appropriately adapted can also lead to a regeneration deficit.

- Not working in periods; a biker has almost the same level of form throughout the year.

- Ignoring the rules of regeneration.

- Increases and leaps in load within the year's structure can result in a stagnation in performance or even a deterioration in performance.

- Training at normal levels in the case of colds or infections often causes a break in performance as well as serious illnesses.

- Nutrition is not in keeping with the load levels.

- Monotony in the training process is frequently a hindrance to performance.

6 HEALTHY BIKING

In the last few chapters you have learnt a good deal about the individual adjustment of a mountain bike and optimal training procedures. Physical problems can still turn up, however; the next few pages will tell you just what you can do to help. You should always be aware of the fact that your body requires a certain amount of time to get accustomed to the unfamiliar position on a new piece of sports equipment. Anyone who takes up biking at 35 onward should go for a detailed medical check-up beforehand.

6.1   Back Problems

Back problems are very often due to an incorrect sitting position. Too much of a difference in height between the saddle and the handlebars can lead to pain around the lumbar area, especially on bumpy routes.

With the front section pointing slightly upward or by having distance rings in the fork stem, it is possible to adjust the handlebars to a higher, more suitable position and thus prevent backache. The sitting distance must also be suitably adjusted.

In any case, when suffering from backache it is necessary to carry out continuous training of both the back muscles and abdominal muscles in particular. As well as this it is necessary to stretch those areas affected.
The tension that newcomers to biking sport and more experienced bikers face at the beginning of the season mostly doesn't last long and disappears again with an improvement in flexibility and performance capacity of the back muscles.

6.2   Neck

Neck problems are also generally due to an incorrect sitting position. Those who don't take an active part in racing sport should by all

Neck pains

Backache

Sunburn

Pains in
the hand,
numbness

swisspower

Sitting
position

Pain in the
knees

Scrapes

Soles of the feet

*Illustration 6.1: Particularly over the first few kilometers, some of
the physical problems illustrated above are almost normal, even the
professionals have to tackle this at the beginning of the season*

Slight flexing

Higher strain

means choose a medium position to prevent neck problems arising; cycling in a stretched position means having your head tucked too far down in the neck. The neck muscles get cramped and and cause pain. Wet tricots or undershirts made of cotton can also trigger off pain due to the skin undercooling. In this case it is recommendable to wear special collars underneath, or functional undershirts with a polo neck.

Illustration 6.2:
Stretched and moderate
position: the angles
between back and neck
alter considerably

6.3 Hands

Pressure marks and even blisters on the palms of the hand can be avoided by wearing cycling gloves. Anyone who is particularly sensitive here should definitely cycle with a softly adjusted fork suspension. A numb feeling in the fingers is also possible after long tours; a smaller difference in height between saddle and handlebars (as described above) will solve this problem as the pressure is taken off the hands. Problems in the wrists are often caused by the same thing but also by an unfavorable, incorrect position of the wrist. Shaped downhill handlebars, Bar Ends or special elastic grips can be altered, changing the angle of the wrist so that the pain disappears.

Illustration 6.3: Downhill handlebars eases the angle of grip. Steering becomes more ergonomic

6.4 Knees

Mountain bikers, as opposed to 'running' athletes, have very few problems with their knees. The knee joints do not have to absorb impact, unlike when running, and they are not exposed to twisting and bruising as they are in may other types of sport. If, however, problems still occur, it is often because the following points have not been heeded.

1. Use low gears.
2. Keep oneself warm.
3. Sitting position (saddle too low).
4. Pedalling system (rigid foot positioning can lead to problems).
5. Bent pedals or cranks.

A more detailed desription of knee problems can be found in the Handbook of Competitive Cycling.

6.5   Feet

When the soles of your feet ache or burn this is generally due to unsuitable shoes. This particularly occurs when cycling with running shoes. The soft shoe sole 'sags' on the pedal and the foot muscles end up with cramp and this is painful. For this reason, mountain bike shoes have a very hard and inflexible sole. The fit of the shoe can also bring on problems e.g. a very narrow shoe for a wide foot. If the pain does not go away after 10 rides within three weeks it is advisable to buy new shoes.

6.6   Scrapes and Grazes Caused by Falls

As far as skin injuries caused by falls are concerned, mountain bikers are mostly confronted with scrapes and grazes. Scrapes are unfortunately part of a racing biker's daily routine, a downhiller's even more so. They mostly occur at the hip (thigh), shoulder, knee (lower leg) or the elbow. The wounds often occur in places, which one sleeps on and which are constantly stretched and bent. Full tetanus protection should be a matter of course. As dirt always enters the wound during a fall, it must be removed again when dressing the wound later. If the wounds are not too deep, it is possible to clean it with disinfectant soap; if it is much deeper then it should be attended to by a doctor. It's always recommendable to spray a cleansed wound with a disinfectant. Smaller cuts can be left uncovered, larger ones need further medical attention.

6.7   The Seat

Inflammation or soreness of the bottom are mainly caused by badly fitting cycling pants. The synthetic leather lining in the shorts must be closely fitted to the bottom without folds. They should normally be washed after every or every second training session, as otherwise germs are rubbed into the sensitive skin and can lead to infection. Not every pair of pants fits every bottom, as the type of seam and type of lining wears to various extents. Once you've found the right make for you, you should stick to it. In any case it makes sense to rub your

bottom with vaseline or, even better, with a special 'sitting' cream. If the seating area is once reddened, it can be treated with e.g. Bepanthene®. Bikers who do a lot of biking usually notice that their bottom gets used to the rubbing. The saddle can also be responsible for seat problems. A harder saddle is better for frequent bikers than a soft one.

6.8   Sunburn

A cycler's skin is exposed to strong sun rays particularly in the summer months. New studies have shown that this radiation on long tours exceeds the recommended maximum values by a significant amount. This is particularly true for tours in higher mountain areas.

One often forgets that a training session over several hours in a short tricot and shorts can cause just as much sunburn as a visit to the beach. In the mountains, ultraviolet rays are considerably higher than on flat land (20-100% more per 1,000m), which can lead to serious burns. Apart from sunburn, ultra-violet rays can also have the following negative consequences for the skin:

1. Ageing of skin
2. Carcinom (skin cancer)
3. Allergic reactions (sun allergy)

For this reason it is necessary in the summer to apply a suitable suncream before heading out on a tour, particularly when one takes into account that there has been an increase in UV rays due to the hole in the ozone layer.

The skin reacts particularly sensitively to sun in the early year training camps (Feb/Mar) in southern regions; it often results in an allergy to the unaccustomed sun irritation.

6.9 That Old Numb Feeling

Nearly every biker is familiar with the problems that one has in the seating area following a long tour. Women also suffer from reversible pains, particularly due to chafing in the genital area.

The high pressure in combination with the many bumps and impacts (trails) can lead to a swelling of the prostate gland, an irritation of the urethra and/or a nerve compression with a numb feeling in the penis and even pain when passing water. Women are mostly confronted with chafing and pressure marks around the pubic bone. These symptoms go away again by themselves.

A new study at the German Sport University Cologne clearly showed that cycling does not have any negative influence on sexual potency. What can be of assistance, as far as the pains are

concerned, is a special, anatomically formed, soft saddle, which leans forward a bit, thicker tires with improved shock absorbence as well as handlebars that are set slightly higher. In addition, one should get up out of the saddle at regular intervals thus giving some relief to the seating area and all the sensitive parts underneath (prostate gland, urethra, nerves, vas deferens).

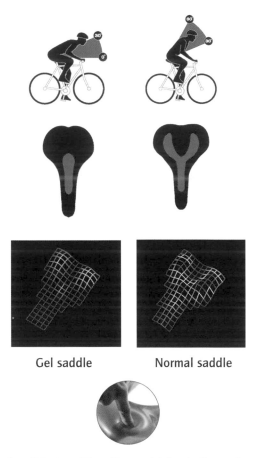

Gel saddle   Normal saddle

Illustration 6.4: A saddle with a gel inlay in the perineum area distributes pressure and can prevent complications better

6.10 Colds

Mountain bikers, due to climatic circumstances, are more prone to catching colds. However, in total they are affected by colds less than non-sporting people. The weather in spring is often bad and one must be particularly careful to protect oneself against colds and infections. Very high training and competition loads can attack the immune system, thus raising your vulnerability to infection. Training with a bad cold or even with a high temperature is taboo, as other organs can end up being affected too (inflammation of the heart muscle).

After recovering from an illness, you should start again very slowly with training; an excessively quick increase in load often results in a state of overtraining. After a bad cold that lasted one week, you require at least 2-3 weeks to reach the level of performance that prevailed before the cold. If you ignore a bout of snuffles it frequently results in chronic paranasal and even frontal sinusitis, which must be completely cured before taking up training again, because such a malady bears the danger of heart damage.

7 VARIOUS BIKING TIPS

7.1 Drinks

On the evening before a long tour, it's not only important to eat enough, the body's fluid intake and output must also be brought into balance. The best thing to do is to drink two or three additional bottles of mineral water during the day so that there's absolutely no chance of starting the tour the next day with a fluid deficiency.

Regular drinking (200ml every 30 minutes) prevents a sudden drop in performance. The hotter the weather is, the more one needs to drink. But there is also a considerable fluid loss in cold weather. The cold air must be moistened in the airways; the colder the weather is, the dryer the air. A drinks bottle with frozen content also enables the biker to take a cold sip in very hot weather. Because not much of this drink comes out there is no need to worry about stomach problems.

Illustration 7.1: Pure water quenches thirst

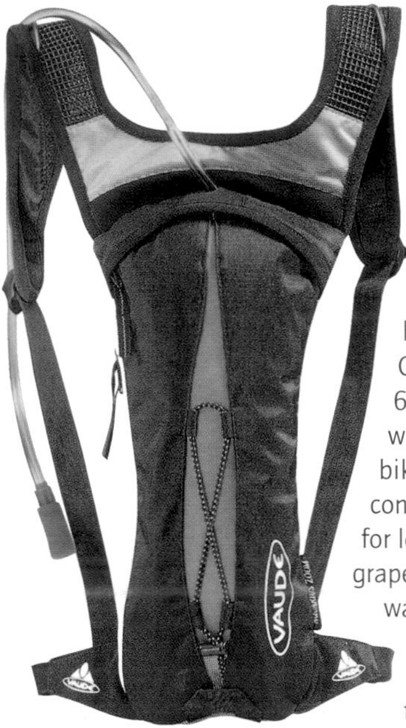

In hot weather, pure water is the best thirst-quencher. Drinks should not be too cold in order to avoid tummy problems.

In order to prolong your performance ability, carbohydrates and minerals should be added to the drink. Ready-made drinks are a good help here as long as they are not too highly concentrated.

Concentration mixes of around 6% (6g carbohydrate to 100ml water) are easy to digest. Very few bikers can manage higher concentration mixes. A good drink for long tours is a mixture of apple or grape juice together with a mineral water of high magnesium content in a 1:1 or 1:2 ratio. In the end it is your individual sense of taste that decides on the choice of a drink.

Illustration 7.2: Handy helper: rucksack for drinks

If you feel very tired, performance capacity can be boosted again with Coca Cola. On long tours in particular, a half-liter of Cola at just the right time enables a biker to continue the tour without any problems. It also temporarily stills a hunger attack.

So-called **drinks rucksacks** have proven to be very handy. While racing cyclists frown upon them, mountain bikers love these 1.5l to 2.5l drink dispensers. It is possible to store a tool, the waterproof jacket and energy bars in them too. Due to the ergonomic belt system you don't notice the rucksack after a few kilometers.

7.2 Food

Bars and Bananas

For every tour lasting over an hour, it is necessary to have in your tricot pocket some snacks with you which are rich in carbohydrates. Energy bars are perfect here; easier again, not to mention being cheaper, are bananas. Slices of cake in tin foil, muesli bars, and low-fat sandwich rolls are just as suitable.

Spaghetti Party

On the night before a big tour, you should throw a so-called **pasta party**. One eats a very big portion of pasta, potatoes or rice with a low-fat sauce. As already mentioned, you must take plenty to drink. On the morning of the tour, a breakfast which is rich in carbohydrates is very important. However, a normal portion is enough here.

Tours over Several Days

When going on tours that go on for a number of days, it is necessary to provide your body with the necessary amount of calories every evening. Usually pasta is eaten.

One should start taking in carbohydrates directly after exercising in order not to lose any time in filling up your reserves. Cola or other drinks that are high in sugar are very suitable; solid foods are often hard to digest.

7.3 Cross-country and Marathon

Once you've been hit with bike fever, you'll soon want to take part in marathons or even in cross-country races.

First Contacts with a Bike Store

Anyone wishing to start out in this area should head to the bike stores, as all the bikers out of that region generally buy their bikes there and one soon gets into contact with others.

Many stores organize tours and training excursions, or the local biker club might have their next training meeting there. At the very least, you will be provided with information on clubs and events.

7.4   Racing Events and the whole Scene

One can find detailed information on the whole biking scene such as racing calendars, marathon dates, news on materials and clothing as well as race reports and tips in the various monthly mountain bike magazines. A list of bike magazines can be found in the appendix as well as a further selection of internet bike-pages.

Marathon
Mountain bike events are referred to as **marathon,** not because they cover a distance of 42.195 km as one would expect. Marathons are generally longer and quite hard. Marathon races take place all over the US or Europe from the end of March to October preferably in low mountain ranges and the Alps. One can choose between different distances offered by the organizing body. The routes follow paths and trails through the surroundings of the particular venue. One can normally choose between distances lasting from 1-6 hous; in kilometers this would mean from 20km to over 100km, depending on the going and ground surface. An average speed of 15-17km/h is perfectly normal for hobby bikers. One does not have to be a member of a club to take part, although one does normally distinguish between hobby bikers and licensed cyclists.

The starting fees are often quite hefty. Having said that, there are drinks and little snacks on offer on the route, sometimes even a T-shirt or a bag. One should take into consideration, however, that the organization of a marathon is very costly.

A biker who wishes to take things a little bit easier should try out the **Country Tours**. They take place on the type of terrain typical for the cycling tourist industry and are organized by cycling sports clubs.

Cross-country Races
One basically differs between races for all-comers and licensed races. Anyone can take part in the former race, provided one feels physically fit and is able to do this from a cycling technique point of view. For the second type of race you require a license and this is only possible when you are a member of a cycling sports club.

Enrolment for a Race

Generally, you have to enrol for a race in order to take part. A task which the enrolling officer is responsible for in the clubs. However, it is also possible to enrol by oneself or enrol at a later date in the novice class for an extra fee. It is best to send in your enrolment for a race in writing (fax, mail or postcard). One must ensure to take heed of the enrolment deadline, which is usually 1-2 weeks before the race itself. Generally, you have to pay an extra fee for enrolments that are sent in after this date.

License Races

If however, one wants to take part in a race in the licensed class immediately, which is something only to be recommended for young beginners, you should ask in the bicycle store for club addresses. Another possibility of finding out club addresses is through the district, city and regional sports federations (in the telephone directory), all of whom are willing to give out information. Finally, you can also find information on local cycling sports clubs from cycling associations of the various states.

You should choose a club, which is as near as possible to your home town in order to be able to participate in training activities. However, there are very few 'pure' mountain bike clubs, but there are always a few bikers in most of the cycling clubs. In the end you have to cycle your mandatory basic kilometers on the roads anyway.

7.5 Being Safe on Terrain

Despite the numerous obstacles and dangerous situations, relatively few accidents actually occur in biking. This is certainly on the one hand due to the fact that there are generally no cars around. As well as this, accidents and falls on softer ground surfaces, unlike on asphalt, seem to cause fewer injuries.

Nevertheless, the potential dangers of mountain biking must be considered and unfortunately a number of serious accidents also occur. By heeding some tips it is possible to reduce the risk factors of biking dramatically, without limiting your fun and enjoyment.